SUPER EXCLAMATION POINT SAVES THE DAY!

By Nadia Higgins • Illustrated by Mernie Gallagher-Cole

The Child's World®

Published by The Child's World®
1980 Lookout Drive • Mankato, MN 56003-1705
800-599-READ • www.childsworld.com

Acknowledgments
The Child's World®: Mary Berendes, Publishing Director
The Design Lab: Design and production
Red Line Editorial: Editorial direction

Design elements: Billyfoto/Dreamstime;
Dan Ionut Popescu/Dreamstime

ISBN 9781614732686
LCCN 2012932874

Printed in the United States of America
Mankato, MN
July 2012
PA02117

About the Author: Nadia Higgins is a children's book author based in Minneapolis, Minnesota. Nadia has been a punctuation fan since the age of five, when she first wrote "Happy Birthday!" on a homemade card. "I love punctuation because it is both orderly and expressive," Nadia says. Her dream is to visit Punctuation Junction someday.

About the Illustrator: Mernie Gallagher-Cole is a freelance children's book illustrator living outside of Philadelphia. She has illustrated many children's books. Mernie enjoys punctuation marks so much that she uses a hyphen in her last name!

My name is Super E. I am an exclamation point. I usually come at the end of sentences. Use me to show surprise, excitement, anger, fear, and other strong feelings.
My name is Howler. I follow Super E. I like to howl with excitement!

There was trouble in Punctuation Junction. Super E could feel it. A bored, floppy feeling ran up and down his line.

"Oh no," said Howler. The monkey cleared his throat. "Drat," he tried again. "Alas. Woe is me. Curses. Yippee. Who-hooo. Zip-a-dee-doo-dah."

Howler couldn't yell sad things, and he couldn't yell happy things.

"I need exclamation points," he sighed.

Where were all the exclamation points? Had they been kidnapped? Were they sick?

This sounded like a job for a superhero.

Super E left for town. He soon saw the trouble being caused by the missing punctuation.

"Super E," Pam the period tried to shout. "My birthday party is a bust."

"Help me, Super E," Karen tried to yell. "My tricks are tanking."

Ta-da?

Go Curtis. You can do it?

"It's no use, Super E," said Curtis. "My swing has no zing."

7

"Hmmmmmm," said Super E. He put on his X-ray goggles. He squinted hard and turned around. Then he stopped short. "No." He took off his goggles. And he put them back on again. "Yes?"

Could it be? The exclamation points were all in bed.

Super E took out his special remote control and released his mini jets. Then he flew those exclamation points right onto the baseball field.

But the exclamation points would not stay straight. They flopped sideways. They folded over. Their dots were all over the place.

"You look like wet laundry," someone called out.

"Exclamation points," said Curtis, "are you okay?"
Ella sniffled. She wiped her nose. "No, were are not okay."
Curtis wrapped her up in a big hug. "What's wrong?" he asked.

"This." She showed him a piece of paper. It was a note from Ms. Prose, the school principal.

"Nobody likes us," Eugene said with a whimper. "So we all went to bed."

"That's just not true," Pansy said. "We do like you. In fact, we need you. We need you for birthday parties . . .

. . . and magic shows . . .

Ta-da!

Watch out!

. . . and all the most exciting events in life."

"We even need you to stay safe," Harry the hyphen added.

"It is just that sometimes you show up at dentist appointments, math tests, and morning announcements," Harry said gently. "And that is too much excitement."

"You're like chin-ups or glitter or hot peppers," Quinn added. "A little goes a long way." The exclamation points were starting to feel a bit better.

"We are the spice of writing," said Super E. And with that, he zapped all those floppy exclamation points with the power of *wow!* a dose of *yippee!* and a bolt of *hi-yaaa!* And the exclamation points felt great again!

"Let's play ball!" Curtis yelled.

The pitch came at him with a *zoooom!*

"Go Curtis!" the crowd yelled. "You can do it!"

Craaaaack! He hit the ball outside the park.

"Thank you, Super E!" he said as he ran the bases. "And thank you, exclamation points!"

FUN FACTS

What a Surprise!

In Spanish, exclamation points are used at both the beginning and end of a sentence. The first exclamation point is upside down. The second one is normal. *¡Qué sorpresa!* (What a surprise!)

Just One, Please

Some people use more than one exclamation point at a time. "That's great!!!!" they might write. But that's just too much excitement for Principal Prose. Use just one exclamation point at a time, please.

Really?!

Once in a while, it is okay to pair up an exclamation point with a question mark. Examples: Are you sure?! Really?! The speaker is excited while asking a question. Notice the order: question mark first, then exclamation point.

What's in a Name?

To exclaim means to shout with feeling. An *exclamation* is the group of words that are shouted. An *exclamation point* is the punctuation at the end of the exclamation. Of course!

Happy 400th Birthday!

How old is Super E? Four hundred, give or take a few years. Use of the exclamation point in written English dates back to the 1600s.